DAFFY DEFINITIONS

by Joseph Rosenbloom
illustrations by Joyce Behr

 STERLING PUBLISHING CO., INC. NEW YORK

Distributed in the U.K. by Blandford Press

Also by Joseph Rosenbloom

Bananas Don't Grow on Trees
Biggest Riddle Book in the World
Daffy Dictionary
Doctor Knock-Knock's Official Knock-Knock Dictionary
Funny Insults and Snappy Put-Downs
Gigantic Joke Book
How Do You Make an Elephant Laugh?
The Looniest Limerick Book in the World
Mad Scientist
Monster Madness
The Official Wild West Joke Book
Polar Bears Like It Hot
Ridiculous Nicholas Pet Riddles
Ridiculous Nicholas Riddle Book
Silly Verse (and Even Worse)

To Lisa Schechtman

Library of Congress Cataloging in Publication Data

Rosenbloom, Joseph.
  Daffy definitions.

  Rev. ed. of: Daffy dictionary. 1977.
  Includes index.
  Summary: Silly definitions for words from aardvark
to zookeeper. E.g., Dead giveaway—a cancelled
quiz show.
  1. Wit and humor, Juvenile. [1. Wit and
humor. 2. Jokes] I. Behr, Joyce, ill. II. Title.
PN6163.R58 1983   818'.5402   82-19323
ISBN 0-8069-7704-3 (pbk.)

Published in 1983 by Sterling Publishing Co., Inc.
Two Park Avenue, New York, N.Y. 10016
The material in this book was compiled from *Daffy Dictionary*
published by Sterling Publishing Co., Inc.
Copyright © 1977 by Joseph Rosenbloom
Published by Sterling Publishing Co., Inc.
Two Park Avenue, New York, N.Y. 10016
Distributed in Australia by Oak Tree Press Co., Ltd.
P.O. Box K514 Haymarket, Sydney 2000, N.S.W.
Distributed in the United Kingdom by Blandford Press
Link House, West Street, Poole, Dorset BH15 1LL, England
Distributed in Canada by Oak Tree Press Ltd.
% Canadian Manda Group, 215 Lakeshore Boulevard East
Toronto, Ontario M5A 3W9
Manufactured in the United States of America
All rights reserved

aardvark
(ARD-vark) Aan aanimal thaat resembles the aanteater.

abash
(uh-BASH) A big party.

abominable snowman
A pesty Eskimo.

accomplish
(uh-KOM-plish) A partner in crime. *(accomplice)*

accord
(a-KORD) A thick piece of string.

account
The husband of a countess.

accountants
(a-KOWNT-ants) Old accountants never die, they just lose their balance.

acorn
Something caused by a tight shoe.

actor
Someone who would rather have a small role than a long loaf.

adhesive tape
A sticky cassette.

ad-lib
A liberation movement for television commercials.

aftermath
The period following algebra.

Alabama elephants
Elephants whose Tuscaloosa. *(tusks are looser)*

alarm clock
(1) A device to scare the living daylights into you.
(2) A convenient invention if you like that sort of ting. (3) Eye opener.

alligator pear
A crocodile couple. *(alligator pair)*

alphabet soup
Eating your own words.

ambition
(am-BISH-un) A get ahead-ache.

amphibians
  (am-FIB-ee-enz) Animals that tell lies.

animal cracker
  (AN-uh-mal KRAK-er) A lion tamer's whip.

announce
  Exactly one-sixteenth of a pound.

ant
  An insect that works hard but still finds time to
  go to all the picnics.

antifreeze
  (an-tee-FREEZ) What happens to your aunt when
  you steal her blanket.

antique
(an-TEEK) Something one generation buys, the next generation gets rid of, and the following generation buys again.

antlers
Deer don't have uncles, just antlers.

apricot
Where an ape sleeps. *(ape cot)*

April showers
Important events in American history—they brought the Mayflowers.

arcade
The drink served on Noah's boat.

arch criminal
Someone who robs shoe stores.

archeologist
(ar-kee-AHL-e-jist) A person whose career lies in ruins.

architect
Noah's profession.

argument
A discussion in which two people try to get the last word in first.

arithmetic
A subject that is hard work because of all the numerals you have to carry.

armor plate
Dishes that knights ate from.

arrest
  The time you take off for relaxation.

art gallery
  Hall of frame.

arthritis
  Twinges in the hinges.

artists
  People who can draw more than their breath.

astronaut
  (AS-truh-nawt) A person who has to be fired before he can work.

atomic bomb
  What makes molehills out of mountains.

Australian Maharishi
  A kanguru.

B-B gun
A very small or young rifle. *(baby gun)*

baby
Mother's little yelper.

babysitter
Someone who is paid to sit on babies.

bachelor
A man who never Mrs. anyone.

back down
The tail feathers of a duck.

bad comedian
A person who can't even entertain a thought.

bad guy
Someone who, on the sands of time, leaves only heel marks.

baker
A person who kneads the dough.

bakery customer
Someone who takes the cake.

baldness
The perfect cure for dandruff.

banana peel
A golden slipper.

band-aid
A fund for needy musicians.

bandleader
Someone who has to face the music.

banker
Someone who is unhappy if he loses interest.

banks
Where rivers keep their money.

Barbary pirate
Someone who cuts people's hair and then charges them too much.

barber
(1) Someone who goes through life getting in other people's hair. (2) The one person to whom everyone takes off his hat.

barber shop
A clip joint.

barefooted criminal
A heel without a sole *(soul)*.

basketball player
Someone who can dribble all the time and still be neat.

bath
The surest way to get into hot water.

bathing beauty
A girl worth wading for.

beach
A place where people slap you on the back and ask how you are peeling.

beauty parlor
A place where women curl up and dye.

bed
A piece of furniture which gets larger at night when two feet are added to it.

bedbug
An undercover agent.

better batter
What you might get if Mickey Mantle married Betty Crocker.

bird house
Home tweet home.

blood bank
Where Count Dracula keeps his checking accounts.

blood test
The most important examination in vampire school.

blooming idiots
Half-witted flowers.

bluebird
A bird that needs constant cheering up.

bombshell
An exploding egg.

boo-boo
A pair of ghosts.

bookworm
The most educated of insects because it eats up knowledge.

boring speaker
(1) A person who has nothing to say and says it.
(2) Someone who never makes a long story short.

borrowed time
Someone else's watch.

bowling
(1) A sport that is supposed to take you off the streets, but lands you in the alleys. (2) A game in which you build yourself up by knocking things down.

boyhood
A young male juvenile delinquent.

budget
   What you cannot do to an immovable object.

bus driver
   Someone who is not afraid to tell everyone where
   to get off.

cactus
Mother Nature's pincushion.

calories
(KAL-uh-reez) A lot of people can't count calories and have the figures to prove it.

calves
The two animals that follow your every step.

Camelot
(KAM-a-lot) Arabian parking lot. *(camel lot)*

campaign
(kam-PAYN) The worst kid in camp. *(camp pain)*

Canadian bacon
Money, in Montreal.

candlemaker
A person who works on wick ends *(weekends)*.

cannibal
(KAN-e-bl) A person who gets fed up with people.

canoe
(ka-NOO) Like a naughty child, it behaves better when paddled.

can opener
Key to the washroom.

cantaloupe
(Kan-tuh-lohp) (1) What you say when you don't want to run away to be married. *(can't elope)*

(2) What a tired horse says to his rider. *(can't lope)*

canteen
(kan-TEEN) A thirst-aid kit.

cap gun
Pistol worn on the head.

carpet
A floor covering that is sold by the yard but worn by the foot.

cattle rustler
  A beef thief.

cemetery
  (SEM-a-ter-ee) A place people are dying to get into.

chargeable
  (CHAR-je-bl) What the toreador does. *(charge a bull)*

charging elephant
  An elephant who uses his credit card.

charm school
  Where witches learn to cast spells.

chatterbox
  Someone who burns the scandal at both ends.

cheerleaders
  The happiest people at a football game.

cheetah
(CHEE-tah) An animal that is not to be trusted.

chicken of the sea
A frightened skindiver.

chicken pox
Playgrounds for poultry. *(chicken parks)*

chickens
The only animals you eat before they are born and after they are dead.

childish game
Any game at which you are beaten.

child psychologists
Young people who know how to handle their parents.

chop-chop
Two karate blackbelts.

Christmas seal
Santa Claus with flippers.

Christmas shoppers
People who are caught up in the spirit of brotherly shove.

cigarette
A bit of tobacco with a fire at one end and a fool at the other.

cinder
(SIN-der) One of the first things to catch your eye when you are traveling next to an open window.

city slicker
A raincoat worn only in town.

classic
A book that everyone praises and nobody reads.

cleanup
Something nobody notices unless you don't do it.

cliff
(1) A pushover. (2) It isn't always easy to tell the difference between a real cliff and a bluff.

clock factory
A place where people are paid to make faces.

C.O.D.
A type of fish brought by the mailman. *(cod)*

cold front
What you've got when you stand with your back to the fireplace.

cold war
A snowball fight.

comedian
A person who knows a good gag when he steals one.

conceit
A case of "I" strain.

Concord grape
A fruit defeated in battle. *(conquered grape)*

concourse
(KAHN-kawrs) A class that teaches how to become a successful criminal.

conductor
The musician most likely to get struck by lightning.

conference
(KON-fer-ens) A meeting at which people talk about what they should be doing.

confidence
What you start off with before you completely understand the situation.

confirm
(kon-FIRM) A Mafia-run business organization.

Congressional Record
The U.S. Senate's latest disk.

conscience
That small voice that makes you feel even smaller.

controversy
   (KON-trah-vur-see) A collision between two trains of thought.

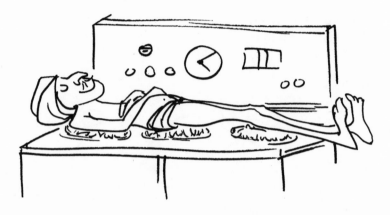

cook
   Someone at home on the range.

cookbook
   A book with many stirring chapters.

corn crib
   Where old jokes sleep.

cosmetics
   (koz-MET-iks) Stuff used by young girls to make them look older sooner, and by their mothers to make them look younger longer.

Count Dracula
   A big pain in the neck.

counterspy
   A store detective.

criminal record
A stolen phonograph disk that contains a long-playing sentence.

criminal shellfish
A mobster lobster.

croquette
(krow-KET) A romantic lady frog. *(croak-ette)*

cross examination
Quiz prepared by an angry teacher.

cross-country skiing
Bad weekend in the mountains.

crow
A bird that never complains without caws *(cause)*.

dandruff
Chips off the old block.

Dark Ages
Knight time.

data
What a baby computer calls its father.

dead giveaway
A cancelled quiz show.

dead ringer
(1) A corpse leaning against a doorbell. (2) A deceased Avon lady. (3) A broken alarm clock.

death
Patrick Henry's second choice.

debate
What lures the fish.

deduce
(dee-DOOS) The lowest card in the deck. *(the deuce)*

deer
Wealthy animal species known for its bucks.

defeat
What you walk on.

defeated politician
Like the earth—flattened at the polls.

deficiency
(di-FISH-en-see) The creatures that live in the ocean.

Defoe
(di-FOH) The enemy author. (Daniel Defoe, 1659?–1731)

degraded
How you feel when you have earned a low mark.

delighted
What happens to a firefly if it backs into a fan.

dentist
(1) A person who gets paid for boring you. (2) The biggest Yank of them all. (3) Someone who can give you the drill of your life.

dentist's office
A filling station.

depth
Height upside down.

detour
(DEE-toor) A road where no turn is left un- stoned.

diamond
There is nothing harder than a diamond, except paying for it.

dictionary
(1) A book in which you can always find health, wealth, and happiness. (2) A guide to the correct spelling of words, provided you know how to spell them in the first place. (3) The one place where Friday comes before Thursday.

diet
A triumph of mind over platter.

dimple
A pimple going the other way.

diplomat
(DIP-luh-mat) A person who can bring home the bacon without spilling the beans.

dirt
  Mud with the juice squeezed out.

dirty double crosser
  A person who sails to Europe and back without washing.

dirty liar
  A musical instrument that needs a good cleaning. *(dirty lyre)*

disk jockey
  Show business personality who lives on spins and needles.

distinct
  How one can tell the difference between skunks and other animals.

Doberman pinscher
The freshest fellow in the town of Doberman.

doctor
Someone who practices medicine but charges as if he knew.

dog
An animal that should never be allowed near a flea circus, because he might walk off with the show.

dog kennel
A barking lot.

dogwood
A tree distinguished by its bark.

double crosser
Someone with a great sense of two-timing.

double-decker bed
A lot of bunk.

double-header
A two-headed monster.

double take
What a pair of shoplifters make off with.

double-talk
A schizophrenic parrot.

down in the mouth
What you get if you bite a live duck.

dragon milk
Milk from a short-legged cow.

draw
The result of a struggle between a dentist and his patient.

dreadful actor
An abominable showman.

dreamer
A man who has both feet planted firmly in the clouds.

dry dock
A thirsty physician.

earth
A minor planet with major problems.

eavesdrop
(EEVZ-drop) What happens when the roof falls in.

echo
What always talks back no matter who you are.

economy
(e-KON-uh-mee) Large size in soap flakes, but small size in automobiles.

egg
A peculiar object; it is not beaten unless it is good.

eggplant
A factory for the manufacture of eggs.

Egg White
Snow White's brother.

electrician
(e-lek-TRISH-an) A person who wires for money.

elephants
The most modest of animals. They always bathe with their trunks on.

elevator operator
A person who is always ready to give others a lift.

engineers
What engines hear with.

Eskimos
(ES-ki-mohz) God's frozen people.

Eskimo shoes
Mush puppies.

Etc.
(et-SET-er-a) An abbreviation used to make people believe you know more than you do.

evaporated milk
The kind of milk preferred by the invisible man.

exact
What eggs do on stage. *(eggs act)*

excess fat
Not the result of the minutes you put in at the dinner table, but the seconds.

exercise
(EKS-er-syze) The only exercise some people get is to: (1) run up bills; (2) wrestle with their conscience; (3) jump to conclusions; (4) stretch the truth; or (5) run out of excuses.

experience
(1) What you have left after you have lost everything else. (2) The wonderful knowledge that enables you to recognize a mistake after you have made it.

expert
An expert is a person who skillfully avoids the small errors only to sweep on to the really big ones.

face lift
An elevator that takes only part of you up.

failure
A person who generally takes the path of least persistence.

false teeth
(1) Like the stars, they come out at night. (2) Many a true word is spoken through false teeth.

farmer
(1) A person outstanding in his field. (2) Someone who works from daybreak to backbreak.

fat
The penalty for exceeding the feed limit.

fat cashiers
Chubby checkers.

fat cat
A flabby tabby.

feather bed
Where feathers sleep.

feed store
The only place where you can get a chicken dinner for 10 cents.

fence
The difference between one yard and two yards.

ferryboat
Something that makes every passenger cross.

fiddler crab
A rather grouchy violinist.

fiddlesticks
What you play violins with.

figurehead
(FIG-yer-hed) Mathematical genius.

firecracker
A hot cookie.

firing line
A dangerous geometric figure.

first aid kit
A cat that works for the Red Cross.

fish
An animal that manages to go on vacation at the same time as most fishermen.

fisherman
(1) A sportsman who sometimes catches a big fish by patience, sometimes by luck, but most often by the tale. (2) A person who often drops the fish a line, but seldom hears from them. (3) A jerk at one end of the line waiting for a jerk at the other end.

fishing tackle
A football player with rod and reel.

flashlight
A case in which to carry dead batteries.

flat face
The result of keeping your nose to the grindstone.

flattery
(FLAT-e-ree) Soft soap, composed of 90 per cent lye *(lie)*.

fleabag
What you carry fleas in.

flea market
Where fleas do their shopping.

flood
A river that has grown too big for its bridges *(britches)*.

flowers
Lazy forms of plant life. They are often found in beds.

fly casting
Lining up flies for parts in a movie or play.

flypaper
(1) Blueprint for an airplane. (2) The best material for making kites. (3) A newspaper read by insects.

forger
(FAWR-jer) Someone who is always ready to write a wrong.

foul ball
Where chickens go to dance.

freak accident
What happened, for example, when the bearded lady ran into the rubber man.

free speech
When you can use someone else's phone.

French bread
Money in France.

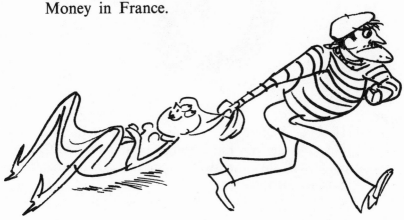

French heel
Low character from Paris.

friar
(FRY-er) A religious young chicken.

Friday
The best day of the week for frying.

friend
One who always excuses you when you have made a fool of yourself.

frog
An animal that croaks all the time but means it only once.

garlic
(GAHR-lik) Vegetable which is excellent for avoiding cold germs. Eat enough of it and people with colds will stay far away from you. Of course, so will other people.

garter snake
A perfectly harmless reptile, but it has been known to snap on occasion.

ghost
A shadow of its former self.

ghost writer
 A spooksman.

giraffe
 The highest form of animal life.

girdle
 (1) A device used to keep an unfortunate condition from spreading. (2) Proof that figures can lie.

goat
 An animal that has the bad habit of butting in.

gold soup
  Soup made with 14 carrots *(carats)*.

good manners
  Making your company feel at home, even though
  you wish they were.

goose
  A bird that grows down as it grows up.

goose pimples
  What a goose gets from eating too much chocolate.

grass
What grows by the yard and dies by the foot.

gravely
How an undertaker speaks.

Great Plains
The 747's.

grouch
One who, when opportunity knocks, complains about the noise.

ground beef
A cow sitting on the grass.

gym dandy
An athlete who wears shirt and tie during a ball game.

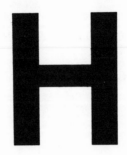

haggle
  A little crone.

half gainer
  Swimmer who diets part of the time.

halo
  (HAY-loh) What one angel says to another angel. (*hello*)

happiness
Happiness is like potato salad: share it with others and you can have a picnic.

hard-boiled eggs
Eggs laid by tough chickens.

harp
(1) A piano in the nude. (2) A giant egg slicer.

hat rack
Torture instrument for headgear.

haunted wigwam
A creepy teepee.

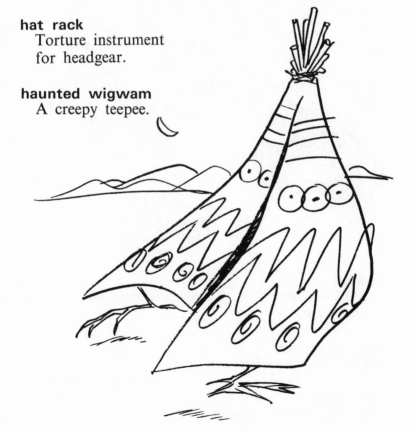

head hunter
The person to see if you have lost your head.

helium
(HEE-lee-um) What a medicine man tries to do.
(heal 'um)

hero sandwich
What brave soldiers eat.

high noon
Midday on Mt. Everest.

historians
(hi-STAWR-ee-anz) People who won't let by-gones be bygones.

hit song
A tune that stops being popular by the time you learn the words.

hobo
A road's *(Rhodes)* scholar.

hog wash
Where pigs do their laundry.

"Home on the Range"
The teapot's favorite song.

hominy
(HOM-in-ee) An unknown number. Ex: Hominy *(how many)* times do I have to tell you to cut that out!

hootenanny
(hoo-ten-AN-ee) What you get if you cross a goat with an owl.

horse
(1) A six-legged animal. It has forelegs in front and two legs behind. (2) An animal that cannot say yes, only nay *(neigh)*.

horse and buggy
Description of an odd person who has laryngitis. *(hoarse and buggy)*

horsehide
What helps keep a horse from falling apart.

horse sense
A quality found most often in persons with a stable mind.

hospital
A place where people who are run down wind up.

hot chocolate
Stolen candy.

hotel
A place where you pay good dollars for poor quarters.

housemother
The question to ask about your female parent's health. *(how's mother?)*

hula dancer
A shake in the grass.

humbug
An insect that wants to sing but just doesn't know the words.

Humpty Dumpty
A camel that won't let you ride him.

ice
Skid stuff.

icy sidewalk
An icy sidewalk is like music, if you don't see sharp *(C♯)*, you'll be flat *(B♭)*.

illegal
A sick bird. *(ill eagle)*

impeccable
(im-PEK-uh-bl) Something chickens can't eat.

Indian reservation
The home of the brave.

indigestion
The failure to adjust a square meal to a round stomach.

insurance
What you pay now so when you're dead you'll have nothing to worry about.

intelligence
A quality clearly shown by anyone who agrees with you.

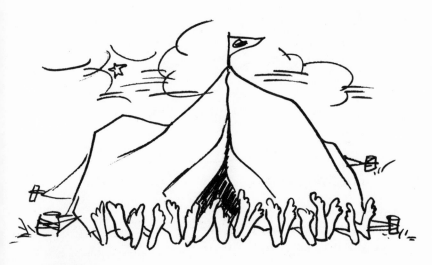

intense
(in-TENS) Where scouts sleep on a camping trip.

jaywalker
   A dumb bird with a short life.

jet-setter
   A fast-flying dog.

Jonah
   The strongest man in the Bible. Even a whale
   could not keep him down.

jungle-gym
   Tarzan's brother. *(Jungle Jim)*

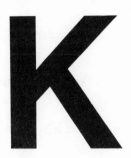

kilocycle
Vicious bike. *(killer cycle)*

kindergarten teacher
Someone who knows how to make the little things count.

kith and kin
To show much affection.
Ex: I kith *(kiss)* her when I kin *(can)*.

Kleenex
A daily nose-paper *(newspaper)*.

knapsack
Where the Sandman keeps his supplies.

knife sharpener
A man who is busiest when things are dullest.

knotty pine
The craziest tree.

know-how
Ability to speak an American Indian language.

kooky
A small, sweet cake that goes very well with milk. *(cookie)*

lap
What you lose every time you stand up.

Lapland
Thinly populated area in Northern Europe. There are not many Lapps *(laps)* to the mile.

Laplander
Someone who is unable to keep his balance on a crowded bus.

large-scale
What a fat person weighs on.

lattice-work
What salads do for a living.

laughing stock
Cattle with a sense of humor.

launch
The meal most favored by astronauts. *(lunch)*

lawsuit
Uniform worn by a police officer.

lawyer
(1) Someone who prepares a 10,000 word document and calls it a brief. (2) Old lawyers never die, they just lose their appeal.

layer cake
A sweet food preferred by chickens.

lazy bones
A skeleton that doesn't like to work.

leap year
The best time for a kangaroo.

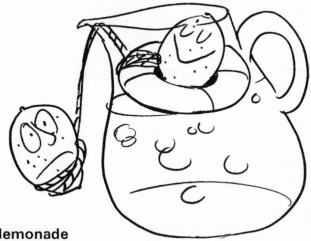

lemonade
To help out a lemon in trouble.

leopard
An animal easy to spot.

Liberty Bell
A perfect name for someone who is half-cracked.

library
The tallest building in the world because it has the most stories.

life
Life is like a shower: one wrong turn and you are in hot water.

life cycle
A bicycle you never outgrow.

light heavyweight
A boxer on a starvation diet.

lightning
The difference between lightning and electricity is that we have to pay for electricity.

light sleeper
Someone who sleeps on the chandelier.

Lincoln's Gettysburg Address
The last one on record is 128 Main Street.

lisp
When you call a spade a thpade.

litter
Our grossest national product.

little things
It is the little things in life that annoy us: we can sit on a mountain but not on a tack.

lobster
A sea creature that plays tennis.

locomotive
(loh-koh-MOH-tiv) A crazy reason for doing something.

Lone Star State
A country with only one actor in it.

long playing record
The most time anyone has ever lasted in a single game.

long puss
What a cat looks like after it has been run over by a steam roller.

long speech
A talk that can make you feel dumb on one end, numb on the other.

Los Angeles Dodgers
Pedestrians in a large California city.

lots
What a real estate salesman has to know.

low-down chiseler
A short sculptor.

mammal
(MAM-al) Something that is neither fish nor fowl.

man
The only animal that goes to sleep when it is not sleepy and gets up when it is.

mayor
(MAY-er) A female horse. *(mare)*

meantime
(1) Nasty watch. (2) Hate *(eight)* o'clock.

meatball
Where butchers dance.

meddler
(MED-ler) Someone whose business is none of his business.

medicine show
Where pills go for entertainment.

medieval
(mee-dee-EE-vuhl) Only half bad.

meow
A catty remark.

metronome
Hollywood elf. *(Metro gnome)*

military dog
A West Pointer.

mind one's business
There are two reasons why some people don't mind their own business: (1) no mind; (2) no business.

mind reading
An easy thing to do—except where the print is too small.

minimum
A tiny English mother.

Minnehaha
(MIN-ee-hah-hah) Small laugh. *(mini ha-ha)*

Minute Waltz
Music played by a watch band.

mischief
(MIS-chif) An Indian chief's daughter.

miser
(MY-zer) A person who lives poor so he can die rich.

misprint
Queen of the Press. *(Miss Print)*

missing link
A stolen sausage.

mistletoe

(MIS-el-toh) What astronauts get instead of athlete's foot. *(missile toe)*

mobile home salesman

A wheel-estate dealer.

modern art

Oodles of doodles.

molasses

(moh-LAS-iz) Additional young girls.

money

(1) Money is often confused with dough. This is not correct, since dough sticks to your fingers. (2) Money talks as much as ever, but what it says makes less cents these days.

monkey business
A swinging corporation.

moonbeams
What holds the moon up.

moonlighting
The sun's other job.

motel
(moh-TEL) William Tell's brother.

moth
An insect that enjoys chewing the rag.

motorists
People who keep pedestrians in running order.

mountain climber
A person who wants to take just one more peak.

mountaineers
(mownt-uhn-EERS) How a mountain hears.

mountain range
A stove designed for use at high altitudes.

mudpies
Organized grime.

muenster cheese
(MUNS-ter cheez) Frankenstein's favorite sandwich. *(monster cheese)*

mufflers
What keeps cars warm in winter.

mumbo jumbo
A mute elephant.

mushroom
The place where they store the school food.

musician
Someone who makes a living by playing around.

mynah bird
(MY-nah bird) Any bird under 18 years of age.
(minor bird)

73

nail

(1) A slender round object with a flat head which you aim at while you hit your thumb. (2) Some people cut their nails and throw them away; others file them carefully.

neurotic cow

An animal that suffers from a fodder *(father)* complex.

Newton's Law
   One fig to every cookie.

night crawler
   Sleepless baby.

nightmare
   A horse that keeps late hours.

night school
   A school run by King Arthur for his men.
   (knight school)

night watchman
   One of those people who can make a living without doing a single day's work.

nonsense
An elephant hanging over a cliff with his tail tied to a daisy.

nonstop talker
Someone who comes back from the seashore with a sunburned tongue.

noodle soup
Nourishment for the brain.

notwithstanding
How to win a sitting contest.

nudnik
(NOOD-nik) A naked Santa Claus.

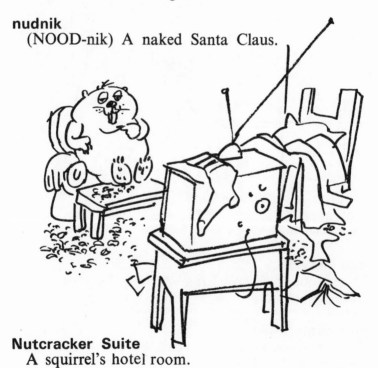

Nutcracker Suite
A squirrel's hotel room.

old comedians
Old comedians never die—they just gag a lot.

old hot rod
A shot rod.

old-timer
A grandfather clock.

open house
Home without a roof.

open mind
Some people think they have an open mind when it is merely vacant.

opera
A musical performance in which people sing before they die.

operator
Someone who hates operas. *(opera hater)*

operetta
A girl who works for the telephone company. *(operator)*

opinion
(uh-PIN-yon) Something you have on your mind and want to get off your chest.

opportunity
It is supposed to knock, but it has never been known to turn the knob and walk in.

optimist
(OP-tim-ist) (1) A man who goes downstairs with a fish pole when he finds his basement flooded. (2) One who spends his last dollar to buy a money belt. (3) A person who goes into a restaurant with no money and figures on paying for his meal with the pearl he hopes to find in the oyster he plans to order.

orange
A fruit with a lot of appeal.

oriental fans
Chinese movie buffs.

osmosis
(oz-MOH-sis) How Moses introduced himself to Pharaoh. *(I'm Moses.)*

ouch
The sound heard when two porcupines kiss.

pancake
A waffle with the treads removed.

pancake make-up
To settle a fight over the breakfast table.

panhandler
(1) A plastic surgeon. (2) A dishwasher.

pants
(1) Golfers wear two pairs of pants in case they get a hole in one. (2) In hot weather a man takes off his jacket, a dog just sits and pants.

parachute school
A school in which you have to drop out in order to graduate.

paratrooper
The only person who can climb down from a tree that he never climbed up.

parole
A word that makes sentences shorter.

pastor
　　To slip by. Ex: She was only a minister's daughter, but you couldn't get anything pastor *(past her)*.

patience
　　The ability to idle your engine when you feel like stripping your gears.

peach
　　An apple in need of a shave.

pea jacket
　　What a pea wears to keep warm.

pen
The pen is mightier than the sword, because no one has yet invented a ball point sword.

penguin
A bird that dresses formally on every occasion.

pen pals
Pigs who are fond of each other.

perfect timing
Being able to turn off the "hot" and "cold" shower faucets at the same time.

perfume
(1) A gift that can cost a pretty scent. (2) An odor that leaves you smell-bound. (3) A best smeller.

personal foul
A chicken of your very own.

pessimist
(PES-i-mist) (1) A person who finds bad news in fortune cookies. (2) Someone who hangs around delicatessens because he is always expecting the wurst *(worst)*. (3) A person who looks at a doughnut and sees nothing but the hole.

petty officer
A naval officer in charge of unimportant matters.

photo finish
Graduation picture.

photographer
A confused person. First he asks you to smile, and then he snaps at you. The worst kind acts friendly enough, but then blows you up.

physician
(fi-ZISH-an) Someone who loses patients if he loses patience.

piano chord
What you tie a piano up with.

pickle
A cucumber turned sour because of a jarring experience.

piemaker
A person whose job takes a lot of crust.

pigeon-hole
A bird's apartment.

piggy bank
Where pigs keep their money.

pioneer
(PYE-uh-neer) What a sloppy pie eater gets. *(pie in ear)*

pipe dreams
What plumbers have when they sleep.

Plymouth Rock
Dance popular among the earlier settlers of the United States.

pocket watch
A watch for people who don't like having time on their hands.

poets
(POH-ets) Writers who are usually poor, because rhyme does not pay.

policeman
Someone strong enough to hold up traffic with one hand.

policeman's ball
A cop hop.

politeness
Yawning with your mouth closed.

political candidate
A person who stands for what he thinks the people will fall for.

politician
(pahl-uh-TISH-un) (1) A kind of acrobat. He has to straddle the fence, keep his fingers on the pulse of the nation, point with pride, look to the future, and keep both ears to the ground. (2) A person who thinks twice before saying nothing.

poll taker
Someone who steals poles.

polyclinic
(PAHL-ee-klin-ik) A hospital for sick parrots. *(Polly clinic)*

polygon
(PAHL-ee-gon) A disappearing parrot. *(Polly gone)*

polysyllables
(pahl-ee-SIL-a-blz) How a parrot speaks.

polyunsaturated
(pahl-ee-uhn-SACH-uh-ray-ted) A dry parrot.

Pony Express
The fastest way to ship young horses.

pop fly
A father insect.

postage stamp
A persistent piece of paper. It sticks to one thing until it gets there.

postman
A job that takes a lot of zip.

post office
Two words that have thousands of letters in them.

potholder
Someone clutching his belly.

pot roast
A sunburn on the stomach.

poverty
You know you are really poor when the only thing you can pay is attention.

prehistoric times
The most widely read newspaper in the Stone Age.

pressing engagement
Two tailors who plan to get married.

pressure cooker
Someone who works in a busy restaurant.

pretzel
(PRET-sel) A snack for someone with a twisted mind.

pretzel maker
The only person who makes crooked dough and is never arrested for it.

prickly pear
Two porcupines going steady.

private eye
What you keep under an eye patch.

prize-fight
Disagreement over what's inside the crackerjack box.

psychic
(SYE-kik) Someone who charges medium prices.

psychopath
Crazy road.

public speaker
Someone who believes in a wordy *(worthy)* cause.

public speaking
The art of making deep noises from the chest sound like important messages from the brain.

pull
What a dentist needs in order to be successful.

quack
A doctor who treats sick ducks.

quadruplets
Four *(for)* crying out loud.

quarterback
Your change from a dollar when you spend seventy-five cents.

quartz
There are four to a gallon.

quick-change artist
A supermarket clerk who can take your money, give you change, and sketch your portrait at the same time.

R

rabbit farm
A hare-raising
(hair-raising)
place.

racketeer
(rak-uh-TEER) A dishonest tennis player.

ragtime
When your clothes wear out.

raisin
A worried grape.

rap session
A mummy's convention.

raving beauty
A girl who thinks she was cheated in a beauty contest.

reckless
(REK-les) Someone who has driven a car for years without a single accident.

red letter day
When the citizens of Moscow get their mail.

revolving door
A good place to meet people and go around with them.

river bank
Where fish keep their money.

roadbed
Where the highway sleeps.

road hog
A pig who hitch-hikes.

rock'n'roll
Bulldozer's breakfast.

rock festival
A special celebration for geologists.

rocket
What you do to a baby to put it to sleep. *(rock it)*

rodeo performer
Someone who makes a living by throwing the bull.

roll call
Mating sound of a sesame seed bun.

rooster
An alarm cluck.

rotisserie
(roh-TIS-a-ree) A ferris wheel for chickens.

royalty
People who get their jobs through relatives.

sale
Where people go bye-bye.

Samson
The most popular actor in the Bible. He brought the house down.

sandwich
Seashore sorceress. *(sand witch)*

school board
The principal's paddle.

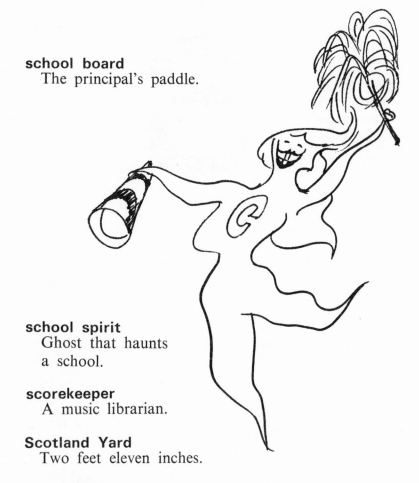

school spirit
Ghost that haunts
a school.

scorekeeper
A music librarian.

Scotland Yard
Two feet eleven inches.

scrap book
A book that tells you how to fight.

scratch paper
Paper that makes you feel itchy.

screen door
What kids get a big bang out of.

screen test
Something that insects are always trying to pass.

screwdriver
The nut behind the wheel.

sculptor
A chiseler. However, a sculptor who needs a bath is the worst kind, because he is a dirty chiseler.

seashell
A torpedo.

seasickness
What a doctor does all day.

seasons
Everyone has a favorite season. Winter, however, leaves some people cold.

season tickets
Tickets the police hand out to bad drivers in order to save all that paper work.

seat belt
What you get if you stand too close to an irritated donkey.

secret
Something you tell to one person at a time.

serious discussion
A case of mind over chatter.

serum
(SEER-um) Note if any place is available. Ex: Do you serum *(see room)* for me in the lifeboat?

sheet music
(1) What ghosts read to keep up with the latest tunes. (2) Music composed in bed.

sheik-to-sheik
A dance for Arabians.

shooting star
A famous actor who uses his gun too often.

shotgun
A worn-out firing piece.

show-off
A clear case of mistaken non-entity.

shutter bug
An insect that likes to take pictures.

shy person
Someone who must pull down the shade to change his mind.

sickbed
The perfect place for a sleeping pill.

sickle
Just a little bit sick.

sidewalk
Something that wears shoes but has no feet.

skiing
A winter sport learned in the fall.

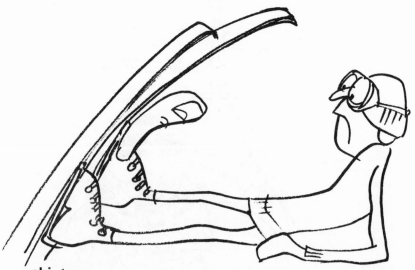

ski tow
(1) What skiers get instead of athlete's foot.
(2) Short for a nasty little bug that bites. *('squito)*

sleeping bag
A knapsack *(nap sack)*.

smash hit
A broken phonograph record.

smiles
(1) The longest word in the English language because there is a mile between the first and the last letters. (2) Curves that straighten most things out. (3) Inexpensive way to improve your looks.

snapdragon
A long fire-breathing monster with a short temper.

snappy answers
What you would get if you crossed a telephone and a lobster.

sneakers
Footwear for spies.

snoop
Someone who believes there's no business like your business.

snoring
Sound sleeping.

snowball
Where snowflakes go to dance.

snowbank
Where Eskimos keep their savings.

snow job
Snowman's occupation.

soap and water
What makes criminals come clean.

soap opera
Singing while taking a bath.

song writer
(1) Someone who may not be able to carry a tune, but surely knows how to lift one. (2) A person who was calm and composed.

sourball
A dance for lemons.

spaghetti
A food discovered by a person who used his noodle.

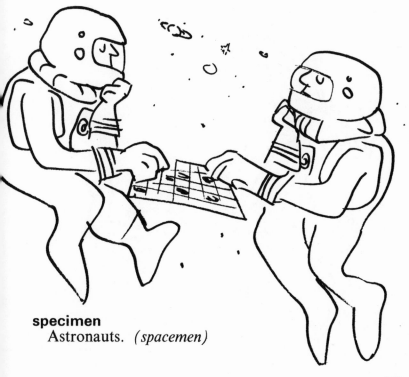

specimen
Astronauts. *(spacemen)*

speechmaker
One who talks while others sleep.

spellbinder
A magician's looseleaf notebook.

spelling
The most important subject a young witch learns in school.

spelling bee
An insect that gets high grades in English.

spice
More than one spouse.

spitting image
Disrespectful statue.

stage manager
A Wells Fargo driver.

stalemate
A boring spouse.

Stamp Act
Temper tantrum.

standing army
Cheaper to maintain than a regular army because you don't need chairs.

statesman
(1) A person who watches his appease and accuse *(p's and q's)*. (2) Someone who can be disarming, even though his country isn't.

steel wool
What gangster sheep do.

steering committee
Two backseat drivers.

stingy person
A person who won't even tip his hat.

stir-crazy
Mad chef's symptom.

stock exchange
A place where you trade in your old cattle.

stopper
To prevent a girl or woman from doing what she wants. Ex: She was only a bottlemaker's daughter, but nothing could stopper *(stop her)*.

striking personality
A prize fighter.

sunbath
A fry *(fly)* in the ointment.

sunburn
Getting more than you basked for.

sunspots
Interplanetary measles.

supernatural
How monsters behave when they are relaxed and just themselves.

surfer
(SURF-er) Man over-board.

surgeon
(1) A big operator. (2) Like comedians, they keep people in stitches. (3) Old surgeons never die— they just cut out.

sweater
Something you put on when your mother gets cold.

sweepstakes
A lottery for janitors.

sweets
People who eat sweets end up with big seats.

swell
To see something swell, hit your thumb with a hammer.

swinger
A pendulum.

synonym
(SIN-uh-nim) A word you use when you can't spell the other word.

take the rap
  Hang up a guest's coat.

tapeworm
  What you get from eating cassettes.

Tarzan
  The world's first swinger.

tattletale
(1) Someone with a good sense of rumor. (2) One who doesn't go without saying.

taxi driver
A man who makes a living by driving people away.

teeny weeny
A rather small hot dog.

telephone booth
A yak-in-the-box.

tequila
(te-KEE-la) To murder a female. Ex: He never meant tequila *(to kill her)*.

terrarium
Where monsters work out.

test pilot
Student who comes through exams with flying colors.

third degree
A diploma awarded to convicts.

thirteen o'clock
Time to have your clock fixed.

The Three Little Bears
A story about three nude midgets.

thumb tacks
A tax on hitch hikers.

thumber
(THUM-er) The warmeth theason. *(summer)*

Tibet
   (ti-BET) To gamble on a sporting event.

Tibetan
   (ti-BET-un) To go to sleep. Ex: Early Tibetan
   (to bed and) early to rise.

time
   An excellent healer but a poor beautician.

timid soul
   A person who will leave pussyfoot prints on the
   sands of time.

timpani
   (TIM-puh-nee) A long musical composition.
   Beethoven wrote nine of them. *(symphony)*

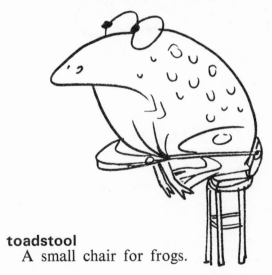

toadstool
   A small chair for frogs.

toe dance
A ball for tow truck operators.

tomorrow
One of the greatest labor-saving devices of today.

tongue depressor
What makes your tongue feel sad.

tongue sandwich
Food that speaks for itself.

totter
(TAHT-er) To educate a female. Ex: I totter (*taught her*) everything she knows.

traffic light
A trick to get you halfway across the road before the cars start coming.

transparent
Mother or father of the invisible man.

trapeze artist
Someone who won't last very long without the gift of grab.

treble
(TREB-l) What musicians get into if they break the law.

tree surgeon
(TREE SER-jun) The only sort of doctor who can fall out of his patient.

tricycle
A tot rod.

trouble
Opportunity knocks only once. Trouble is more persistent.

truth
Stranger than fiction, but not as popular.

tulips
(TOO-lips) What you pucker up with.

turtle soup
A snappy dish.

TV dinner
A meal that comes complete except for the TV.

twitch
A jittery sorceress.

two square feet
What a land surveyor stands on.

two-thirty
The time to visit your dentist. *(tooth-hurty)*

tyrant
(TY-rant) An insect dictator.

U.C.L.A.
What you can observe on a clear day in southern California. *(You see L.A.)*

unbreakable toy
An object which is indestructible—until a child plays with it.

underground garage
A wall-to-wall car pit.

undertaker
(1) A man who puts every customer in his place.
(2) A person who always carries out what he undertakes.

unfinished dictionary
A dictionary that stops at "nothing."

unwelcome visitor
One whose shortcoming is his long staying.

used car
An automobile in first-crash condition.

vanishing cream
  What the invisible man puts in his coffee.

vertigo
  (VER-te-goh) In which direction did he head? Ex:
  He was just here, vertigo *(where did he go)*?

vicious circle
  A round geometric figure with a nasty temper.

vine
A weak plant, since it can't even support itself.

violin
A dreadful little hotel. *(vile inn)*

violinists
The least serious of musicians. They are always fiddling around.

violins
Blood and gore. Ex: There is too much violins *(violence)* on television.

volcano
A mountain that has blown its stack.

wagging tail
A happy ending.

waking up
A question of mind over mattress.

watchmaker
Someone who works overtime.

water bed
Where fish sleep.

watts
How you feel about a light bulb. Ex: I wike this wight bulb watts and watts *(lots and lots)*.

wedding ring
A one-man or one-woman band.

wheeler dealer
An automobile tire salesman.

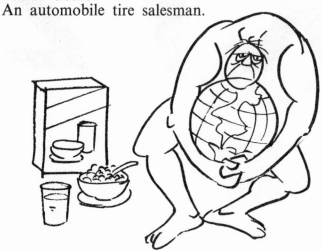

wicker
Drained of energy. Ex: I feel wicker *(weaker)* when I don't have a good breakfast.

wise crack
An educated hole in the wall.

wisecracker
A smart cookie.

witchcraft
A flying broomstick.

wrong
A word that if pronounced right is wrong, but if pronounced wrong, is right.

XYZ

x-ray
Bellyvision.

XX
Treachery or betrayal. *(double-cross)*

yardstick
(YAHRD-stik) Something that has three feet but can't walk.

yawn
(1) An honest opinion openly expressed. (2) Things are always dullest before the yawn *(dawn)*.

YY
Overly smart or clever. *(too wise)*

zinc
(ZINK) Where one puts the dirty dishes.

zing
What you do with a zong. *(sing)*

zoo
A place where people go and animals are barred.

zookeeper
A critter sitter.

INDEX